contents

introduction   iii

40 days of praying with my pen   1

prayers and prompts for holy week 83

acknowledgments 100

index of scriptural praying prompts 100

a teenager hands me a piece of folded notepaper, the outside of which reads simply, "Pastor Rachel, can you give this to God?" As I unfold her note, a handwritten prayer appears, the angst of an adolescent poured out to God in pen.

Around a table in a local café, six heads bow in prayer . . . over the lined pages of journals, with pencils and pens at work. Some write quickly in response to the praying prompt that I have just given them. Others' written prayers fill the paper more slowly: words, phrases, shifting trains of thought, all seeking God.

In the midst of a thorough spring cleaning at home, I am surprised to unearth the traces of my own prayer life from the past year. There within piles of bills, church bulletins, and my kids' school artwork are snippets of prayers that I wrote on whatever was handy.

> *Spin me in circles, Holy Spirit,*
> *and set my feet on a new path.*

prayed on the back of the blue envelope of an electric bill.

> *God, don't let go*

written on a homework sheet recycled as scrap paper.

> *God, bless me with a word*
> *or else bite my tongue to stay silent*

jotted on a paper napkin; I must have written that prayer on a Saturday evening while prepping Sunday's sermon.

For years, it has been my spiritual practice to articulate prayers through my pen, a habit I began after spending my youth and young adulthood convinced that I lacked the discipline for prayer. I never had a model prayer life: my mind wandered aimlessly during mealtime grace, my early morning prayers lacked time and commitment to pray for the whole world, and my bedtime prayers put me to sleep.

Then my son was born in 1999, and I wanted to wrap him with a prayer and a blessing as tightly as I wrapped his swaddling blanket. The words of such a prayer needed to be well-chosen and purposefully crafted. I sat down with pen and paper one afternoon while my son napped, and I wrote:

> *Child of my womb,*
> *the pains of labor are overshadowed*
> *by the joy of hearing your new cry.*
>
> *Nuzzle at my breast, blessed one.*
> *Feed on the warmth of our nearness*
> *as I marvel at your presence.*
>
> *I anticipate my own fear in the days ahead.*
> *You are mine but no longer of joined flesh;*
> *I cannot forever harbor you in my arms.*
>
> *May the angels guard you and guide you.*
> *May the LORD hold you in his right hand*
> *and bless each of your days, firstborn of my children.*

I was hooked. There was a deeply satisfying joy in seeking out the precise words to articulate the prayerful sentiment that I wanted to convey, and a freedom in forming the visual shape of the prayer on paper. Praying by writing took a prayer out of my head and made praying a whole-body exercise: my creativity was sparked, my spirit fully focused, my muscles employed, my sense of touch and awareness of breath heightened. I felt more connected to prayer than I had ever experienced . . .

. . . and more imaginatively connected to the mystery that is God. As I began writing more of my prayers "in longhand," my vocabulary for God expanded. Watching the sun rise into a clear blue sky on the morning after a blanketing blizzard, my pen and spirit identified God as the Eternal Hope of spring. Praying through my impatience with war, God became the Pregnant Mother laboring to deliver a day of peace. The creative possibilities for using words to draw closer to the Word Made Flesh increased my attentiveness to recognizing God within the details of life.

My prayer-writing continued, and I learned that I could attend to my conversation with God almost anywhere as long as I had blank paper in front of me and a pen in hand. So I prayed while sitting in a coffee shop during the noisy morning rush (a frequent and favorite perch of mine). I prayed while watching my kids' soccer practices on cooling autumn evenings, or when taking a break from pastoral busyness to be still in the church sanctuary. I prayed bits of prayers in the margins of my agenda at a church council meeting, or in an unlined journal while relaxing at the beach on a family vacation.

Despite the flexibility of praying with my pen in almost any venue, in actuality my praying habits were still scattered and irregular. I loved writing prayers but felt guilty when I did not do so daily or even weekly. I had long since overcome my reservations about praying aloud in front of others (public prayers and blessings are frequent duties in pastoral ministry), yet I had lingering hang-ups in my personal prayer life: excuses of time or fatigue, responsibilities to family and church, not to mention that the Spirit of my prayers and the Muse of my pen did not always stir on cue . . . especially in the typical pre-dawn "devotional hour" that I felt ought to be devoted to prayer but was, in fact, devoted to whatever winks of sleep I could catch. So, one spring for Lent, I challenged myself to add a daily rhythm to my prayer-writing to regularly practice the penning of prayers that I enjoyed but for which I lacked (or believed that I lacked) serious time.

Writing daily prayers during Lent began as an idea that fell out of my mouth during a church meeting in January 2009. A committee was brainstorming ideas for the upcoming Lenten season, with the goal of increasing the prayer life of each congregant and of the church as a whole. The primary avenue would be small groups, including a prayer-writing small group that I formed; then I suggested an additional forum for prayer—almost before I realized that I had said anything. (Thank you, Spirit.) "I could write a prayer on my blog each day for Lent." I had entered the blogging world in the summer of 2008 under the blog title *Faith and Water*, with the very modest goal of posting at least once per month. Daily blog posts would be a significant change. "At least half of our congregants are online; we'll spread the word through the newsletter and Sunday bulletins that people can find a new prayer on my blog each day to use in their personal Lenten devotions."

Ash Wednesday arrived and Lent began. I wrote prayers for my blog at all times of day—in the morning while my kids ate breakfast, in the middle of the day between meetings, at 2 AM during the night when sleep was evasive. I jotted down prayers after visits to the hospital or the courtroom, in the midst of sending e-mails or writing sermons. For the six and a half weeks of Lent, I penned (then typed) prayers daily at *Faith and Water*, and members of my congregation and of the community prayed with me from their laptops and desktops and smartphones. As I practiced my embodied prayers daily, I began to let go of the worry that my prayer discipline was insufficient and to simply enjoy the connection of my whole self with the Whole and Holy One. When the dust of Lent settled and the Easter lilies wilted and the sheer exhaustion of the season caught up with my body, I marveled to recognize that I hadn't just pastored my congregation through the rituals and stories of Lent; I had taken the Lenten journey as well, and my praying pen had facilitated the experience.

As I write today, in the off-Lenten season, I find that Spirit and Muse often meet and collaborate circumstantially, naturally, and I do not try to manipulate them otherwise; I simply pay attention to mind, body, soul, emotion, and experience. These days, my pen prays while I read the day's news online or after a pastoral visit when deep concern for a parishioner compels me to pull my car off the road to write a prayer. I pray when a rhythmic combination of words plays through my mind or when a captivating image begs articulation. Sometimes I sit, pen in hand, at a complete loss for words to write or pray; in those moments, just holding a pen helps me grasp a prayer:

O God . . .

. . . grant me your patience.

O God . . .

. . . grant me your protection.

O God . . .

. . . grant me your peace.

Dear Jesus . . .

. . . please.

Yet when Lent returns again in the liturgical cycle each spring, I harness Spirit and Muse—with plenty of caffeine—and return to the beloved practice of penning my prayers for forty days.

I invite you to do the same: to practice your prayers through daily writing over the next forty days. *Writing to God* is an opportunity to connect your body, mind, and spirit in prayer for a forty-day journey, and it's a chance to discover a new way to pray. In these pages, you'll find a prayer to read for meditation each day followed by a scripturally based prompt to guide your own pen's prayer. If you're writing through the forty days of Lent, this book has additional prayers and prompts specific to Holy Week. I encourage you to let this space for prayer be safe from self-criticism and doubt about your praying skills. (So many of us are easily intimidated by an inner demon whispering that our prayers are not "good enough.") In the space for *Writing to God*, give yourself the freedom to pray without judgment and to be creative with words as you converse with the Word Made Flesh.

Some ideas for your prayer-writing, based on my experiences with written prayer:

1. Actually use a pen for your prayers. The temptation, when using a pencil, is to erase frequently as part of the writing process. If you find

yourself erasing words regularly (or crossing out penned words left and right), it's likely that your doubts and self-criticism are overtaking your prayer.

2. When your praying pen feels stuck, or you're too worried about writing a "good" prayer to make a mark on the page, write something — *anything*. Doodle in the page margin to check your pen's ink flow. Write two-word descriptions of what you smell, see, and hear at that very moment. Then get back to praying.

3. When you read the Scripture passage and the praying prompt, pay attention to your soul's response to the words: a strong emotion, a resonance with a certain phrase, an image, a memory. Let your prayer flow from those initial responses.

4.   Remember that this is prayer, not poetry or prose or an essay or a letter. Your prayer might look like a list of words one day and a paragraph the next day. Use whatever literary form (or lack thereof) feels most comfortable and most prayerful to your pen. You are even free to skip the traditional "Dear God" salutation:

> *The honeysuckle flowers are blooming*
> *and I am reminded (again)*
> *that Life's surprising joys,*
> *in cycles of hibernation and renewal*
> *are not dependent on my successes or failures.*

Trust that God "hears" your written prayer in any format!

Praying through your pen is not about finding the right or perfect words for prayer; it's about connecting your whole self in an act of physically produced prayer. It's about practicing prayer daily in the safety of a book's pages. It's about exploring the fullness of words as you journey with Jesus through the trials and passions and joys of life. It's about enjoying your conversation with the Holy, creatively, freely, sincerely, in mind, body, and spirit.

Be blessed by the prayers of your pen!

40 DAYS OF PRAYING WITH MY PEN

1 Caffeine

Wake up!
Wake up, my soul,
from your winter slumber
and stretch your tired limbs to savor this season

Shake off your routines like bedcovers
Plant your feet on the ground
for the journey

Clear your eyes of sleep
Take in the sight of a new day
for loving your God

Feast on prayer and scripture
Attend to the holy in life and in love
Do not be weary

Wake up!
Wake up, my soul,
to experience your greatest joy
Be actively present in this day, in this season

God will refresh your spirit.

READ Ezekiel 37:1–3.

What "dry bones" in your life need a breath of fresh air, a burst of new life, from the Spirit? Let your written prayer be God's words of encouragement to you as you let God dust off the dry and weary places of your spirit.

Daily Blessing

God be the light in my eyes.
God be the love in my voice.
God be the gentleness in my steps.
God be the compassion in my touch.
God be the word on my lips.
God be the strength for my spirit.
God be the ground under my feet.

God gives you unique gifts for this day
and this season.

READ Ephesians 6:10–18.

The author advises readers to make full use of the gifts and "armor" of God to live their days fully, confident in faith, wise in the Spirit. What gifts of the Spirit do you need for this day, for this season in your life? Let your written prayer wrap God's strength and grace around your day.

Humility

I pray that you have a sense of humor, O God:

How fickle I am on any given day!
Saddened, thoughtful, worried in one minute
and relaxed, top-of-the-world in the next.

How flighty we are as humans!
Outpouring in generosity for one another,
then intensely self-serving and self-focused.

How quick are the days you have given us!
Faster than the grass withering and fading,
the sun races across the sky to mock our sense of time.

I pray that you laugh . . .
and I will try to do the same.

God is above all and in all and through all!

READ Isaiah 40.

Who is like God? What person, what institution or government, what season, what war can possibly outlast God? Let your written prayer praise God for the mystery of God's eternal power.

Psalm 46:10

Be still and know that I am God.

o my God, i pray for the perspective to bear in mind that i am not God; that no amount of planning, no amount of caffeine, no amount of pride can set me in your place; that yours is the wisdom and the bearing that i need most of all.

Be still and know that I am.

o my God, i ask for the calm and the trust to know that your breath is the source of my life; for the faith and the confidence to know that there is a living God though the mountains should fall and the earth tremble, though rivers of tears should flood seas of heartache.

Be still and know.

o my God, i struggle with the weight of all that i don't know, with the worries of all that remains unseen; grant me the quiet peacefulness of lilies waving in the wind, clothed beyond the beauty of Solomon himself; bless me with the joyful focus of a sparrow going about its work simply because another day has dawned.

Be still.

o my God, i am not still but restless, pressing through each day as though it all depends on me; be the voice in silence just as you once whispered to Elijah on Mount Horeb, and call me to task for lacking faith . . . until i let go of the busy noise that i have created.

Be.

o my God, let me be fully what you have created me to be: a reflection of you in words and in silence, in work and in stillness, in community and in solitude; let me be, to your glory.

God will be your quiet strength.

READ Psalm 46.

For many individuals, the discipline of sitting with God in silence is a difficult one. Today, before you write, sit in silent prayer for ten minutes (setting a timer works well). Relax your body; listen to your breathing; let your thoughts come and go. When the ten minutes have passed, let your written prayer reach out to God for stillness to ground you through the day.

Ashes to Ashes Confession

I am worn down today,
fatigued in every muscle
I am not whole,
not even halfway.
It is brilliant, thrilling to be human . . .
oh but I strain against the ashes
the limits.
Heal me, Jesus, with the scars of your own brokenness.
Heal me . . . not to strength or perfection,
but to togetherness
to gentleness
to taking care of these ashes.
Be the wholeness that I am not
and remind this body of ashes
to rest my scars in yours
to live my broken life
fully.

God will comfort you in all seasons.

READ Ecclesiastes 3:1–20.

There are days, years, and seasons sometimes, when our humanity is evident and tangible in very painful ways. Let your written prayer give voice to the aches of your body, whether your issues are of physical health or spiritual fatigue.

6 The Word Became Flesh

To the One who created humanity and walked among us:

Thank you for people—for all people, but today especially I'm thankful for those who radiate love and warmth and meaning into my life. The simplest gifts of shared laughter, a warm embrace, and caring conversation make all the difference in how I see the day.

It's good to know that you laughed and hugged and talked with your friends too. Having a God who was human helps.

Jesus is with you in all of life!

READ John 1:1–5, 14a.

The good news of the Word Made Flesh is that the God of the highest heavens, the Creator of light and life, has walked along dusty roads, tasted the fresh warmth of crusty bread, and shared a cup of wine with friends in full humanity. Let your written prayer invite the Word Made Flesh to be present and real in your day.

7 In Need of Prophets

In the days to come,
will you stretch out your hand and inspire your people,
Spirit of the Living God?
Will you raise up prophets with tongues of fire
to denounce the crimes of war and of hatred,
to protest the lukewarm tolerance of discrimination?
(And will those prophets be us?)
Spirit of the Living God,
will you shake us from our slumbers
with visions of the work that is needed,
the sweat and labor that are necessary
to turn swords into plowshares
(guns, too, and maybe tanks)?
And after the plows have turned the soil,
will you give us courage to melt the metal again,
this time into bells:
huge, loud, clanging bells that we will ring unceasingly
until the harvest of justice is reaped?
Will you, Spirit of the Living God,
in the days to come?

God will guide the way.

READ Habakkuk 2:1–3.

In your written prayer, lift up a current need for social justice and for visionaries to guide the way toward healing and change.

Heartache

O Holy Heartache,
O Open Wound,
I come to you afresh with pain:
bleeding, sore, and tired.
Will you knit flesh back together,
or will you say, "This pain is my presence?"

O Holy Heartache,
O Open Wound,
I have prayed without ceasing for strength,
battled in pursuit of confident faith.
Do not tell me that I have been wrong,
that holiness is in the vulnerability.

O Holy Heartache,
O Open Wound,
I long to find you in the hurt
so that you will carry me to healing;
instead, you have confined me
to this wilderness of heartache.

O Holy Heartache,
O Open Wound,
I am disquieted to discover your weakness,
discouraged that "getting better" may not be the goal.
Be my solace amidst the unknown;
give me courage to keep bleeding.

God will be present in the midst of your pain.

READ James 5:7–11.

Let's be honest: there is no joy in waiting patiently through suffering. Yet as Job and the prophets and the early Christians testify, God surprises us with strength and grace for endurance in all circumstances.

A Lover's Psalm

I love you, O my God,
my joy and my daily delight.
You awaken my senses at every turn—
in caress and the whisper of sweet nothings,
with beauty and warm embrace.
How good it feels to be wrapped in your love—
like the sweetness of a moment,
I do not savor it enough!
Let me be as a lover to you:
blissfully aware of every minute
every intimacy,
grateful for the tenderness
and strength of affection,
pleased to call myself yours
and you mine.

God loves you!

READ Psalm 36:5–9.

Let your written prayer be a response to the deep love of God.

Sing a song of praise
for the wonder of being
for the triumph of standing firm against the wind
for the dizzying pattern of a snowflake's fall

Whisper a song in prayer
for those who are cold
for the unknown cause of ambulance sirens
for the sun to break through the darkness of winter's depression

Sing a song of hope
for the spring that will come
for the miracle of a snowy blanket fading to vibrant green
for the renewed energy and activity inspired by warmer weather

Repeat a song of praise
for the One who can do all things
who knows the design of frost and dances with the wind
who gives us being and teases our senses with the turning of seasons

God the Creator is beautiful and mighty!

READ Psalm 147.

Let your written prayer celebrate the God of all creation, who commands the storms and swirls the winds and calms the waters.

Lament to the Savior

There is a disconnect—a chasm, it seems—
between the brilliant expanse of sun-glittered ocean
stretching out to meet the endless blue sky
and the devastating, shocking news
of a loved one's terminal illness.

The tie-dyed violets and pinks of the hydrangea
are apparently worlds away from
the overwhelming scarcity that follows flood and earthquake
when survival and despair are measured by the minute,
not even the hour or the day.

It has been too long, dear Savior.
Your people cannot wait for the sweet by and by
to bring eternal satisfaction from hunger
or complete comfort from pain.
God With Us, you are needed.

The Spirit of peace and compassion will bind all wounds.

READ Jeremiah 6:14.

Look around you today; watch passers-by and listen to the world's news. As a global community, where do we seem to be lacking Spirit and compassion with one another? In your written prayer, pray for the much-needed work of the Spirit throughout the world—and through you—this day.

Prayer of Names

O God,
if I call you Father,
will you please watch over me and those in my house,
and guard us like a watchman at night?

O God,
if I call you Mother,
may I curl up next to you when I have nightmares,
and will you soothe me when I am sick?

O God,
if I call you Savior,
will you rescue me during hard times
and keep me from rebellion?

O God,
if I call you Lover,
will you keep me company through thick and thin
and encourage my best self?

And God,
if I confess that you are beyond naming,
will you please be greater than me and beyond my understanding,
so that the things I cannot fathom but so desperately want—
lion-and-lamb peace,
feeding miracles by the millions,
tears-into-joy justice—
can be conceived and built by your imagination?

Will you please be holy so that I can be human,
to the best of my ability?

The Wonderful Counselor will uphold you.

READ Isaiah 9:6.

What name of God—from this passage or from your journey of faith—resonates deeply with your spirit? Let your written prayer be centered around the name(s) of God that you love.

A Prayer
While Waiting
For the Kingdom of God

Give these bones
breath to dance.

Give your people
a song to sing in exile.

Give the mustard seed
roots to grow.

Give Hagar and Ishmael
an oasis to rest.

Give those behind locked doors
a vision of hope.

Give the widow
flour for her bread.

Give the fig tree
fruit to bear.

Give the leper
a temple for his praise.

Give the Easter lily
a reason to bloom.

All heaven and all creation belong to God!

READ Mark 4:26–32.

"With what can we compare the kingdom of God?" There are many mysteries in life, in faith, and in Scripture, as well as unanswerable questions that arise from our experiences. Can you celebrate the unknown expanse of God's imagination? Let your written prayer rejoice that the kingdom of God—on earth and in heaven—is held in God's hands.

Bless the Lord, O my soul,
and celebrate God's beauty
in the diversity of all people made in God's image
in the trees that lift their branches to give God praise
in the birds that greet the Light with their songs

Bless the Lord, O my soul,
and remember God's faithfulness
through storms that overwhelmed me with pounding waves
through deserts where the word of the Lord could not be found
through seasons of planting and harvesting this life that God claims

Bless the Lord, O my soul,
and be joyful on the pilgrimage to God's holy mountain
where neighbors and enemies alike will find common ground
where weariness will not slow our tongues' proclamation of good news
where all people will stand in unity with the poor and imprisoned

Bless the Lord, O my soul,
and bless God's holy name

God plays a hand in every part of our stories.

READ Psalm 78:1–4, 52–55.

We all have stories—testimonies—to tell of our faith journeys. Write a prayer of praise as you reflect on your own testimony, beginning with the phrase, "Bless the Lord, O my soul."

15 Nighttime Prayer

The middle of the night always comes:

I am afraid of the dark

Afraid of the unknown at 2 in the morning

Wide-eyed in case the uncontrollable, unthinkable happens

So I stay awake

Stay distracted

Determined not to be caught off guard by the night

I need you, Lord Jesus,

For this simple act of sleeping

God will comfort you.

READ Isaiah 41:10.

Write a prayer about a fear, and let the presence and encouragement of God surround you with holy comfort.

Recycling: A Prayer for Salvation

Refresh me

Remind me   *Reuse me*

God will renew and revive you!

READ Hosea 6:1–3.

When we are stuck, God can re-imagine our circumstances; when we are tired, God can refresh us; when we are wandering aimlessly, God can refocus us. Let your written prayer invite God to remind you of the miracle of daily resurrections.

17 Unceasing Prayer

I pour out prayers for this day, O Spirit,
like water from a pitcher.

I pray for the breath
to speak words of love and truth.

I pray for the presence
to be mindful and aware of others.

I pray for the wind, filled with signs of spring,
to center me and calm my spirit.

I ask (carefully) for the refiner's fire
to burn away what is unnecessary.

I ask for the energy, the passion,
to do your work well with all of my gifts.

I look for the comfort of the Advocate
to surround and sustain me.

I pray for the covenanted community
to be your witnesses above all else.

Keep my prayers unceasing
and my heart set on you.

God is good!

READ 1 Thessalonians 5:12–24.

Let your written prayer be simple and brief today, a mantra (of sorts) that you can repeat prayerfully throughout this day.

Adoration

Creator God,
you are beautiful in the morning fog when all is gray
you are beautiful in the landscape of rolling hills, steep mountains
*   and cold Adirondack lakes*
you are beautiful in the deep purples, warm whites, and almost-green yellows
*   of cut flowers on my kitchen table*

Creative God,
you are beautiful in the rhythms that resonate through the speakers
you are beautiful in the comforting smell of fresh bread
*   baking in the oven*
you are beautiful in the span of generations, from the wide-eyed wonder of infants
*   to the life-lined smiles of their elders*

Creating God,
you are beautiful in the places where your people are praying
you are beautiful in the work of hands that feed others around the table,
*   around the world*
you are beautiful in the alliances that seek reconciliation
*   across lines of difference and power*

You're beautiful, Creator God,
so very beautiful

Beyond your wildest dream, God is holy!

READ Revelation 4:1–11.

Write your own *sanctus* (hymn of praise; literally "holy"), beginning with the refrain of the mystical creatures and heavenly elders: "Holy, holy, holy!"

Lament

O God, my God, be present in my tears.
I am poured out like water, my heart is like wax.

I pray for the many places of hurt:
—the joint that shoots pain through the body
—the word that undermines trust and love
—the job loss that replaces breath with panic
—the growling hunger in the stomachs of children
—the addiction that devours life and family

O God, my God, do not be too far away to hear.
O my help, come quickly when I groan.

I pray for the open wound:
—the nightmarish memory that haunts the veteran
—the distrust laid brick-by-brick until it is a wall
—the abyss of loneliness that swallows hope
—the emotional fatigue of a chronic physical ailment
—the fear that love will always be lost

Deliver my life from the encircling army.
Rescue your people just as you saved our ancestors.

Give us a story to tell the generations to come
And we will stand in awe, saying the LORD has done it.

Our God is a God who heals.

READ Psalm 22.

Even as the psalmist worries that God is too far away, it's clear that the psalmist also believes God to be Healer and Deliverer. In your written prayer, lift up a need for healing—in your life, in another's life, in the world.

Taking a Breath

Breathe in: You are my God.
Breathe out: And I am yours.

Holy

Holy

Holy Lord

God of all life, be my breath today.

Glory of the morning, be the spark for this small candle.

Breathe in: You are my God.
Breathe out: And I am yours.

Kyrie eleison

Christe eleison

Kyrie eleison

God of mercy, be gentle where I am broken.

Vision of all discernment, be patient where I am stuck.

Breathe in: You are my God.
Breathe out: And I am yours.

Creator

Redeemer

Sustainer

God beyond time, be present in these moments.

Saving Grace, be endless generosity through my finiteness.

Breathe in: You are my God.
Breathe out: And I am yours.

You belong to God.

READ Exodus 6:5–8.

Sometimes when we are groaning with stress and worry, we forget to breathe deeply. Let your written prayer release the strain from your shoulders and the pain from your heart as you savor the good news that you belong to God.

Loving the Holy

Because so often life seems to be without order:
I love you, O Holy One who creates and tells stories.

Because I struggle to understand and tackle the world's injustices:
I love you, O Holy One who promises deliverance.

Because I strive and try and work . . . and then wonder where I'm going:
I love you, O Holy One who guided Hagar and Miriam and Naomi.

Because you do not leave me alone when I need comfort and when I need prodding:
I love you, O Holy One who is restless and passionate.

Because you are not me; because you are beyond this world and still choose to be part of it:
I love you, O Holy One who lights the fire when I need it most.

God is faithful.

READ Hebrews 11:1–12.

Faith is the conviction of things not seen, yet faith is often grounded in past stories of what God has already done, past stories that were witnessed and handed down to us. Let your written prayer celebrate God's faithfulness throughout time, and God's presence with you today.

Emmanuel

So another day ends.
Words have been spoken,
Moments shared.
Comings and goings;
And where am I now?
I am with YOU.

Amazing, what a day can hold.
Events, conversations,
Highs and lows of emotion.
But inevitably all is done;
Enough for today.
And still YOU are with me.

Could I still chart this day in detail?
Probably not.
Where I am forgetful,
I pray that I have not been careless.
One truth is clear in hindsight:
I was with YOU,
And YOU with me.

God will be with you always.

READ Matthew 1:23.

In your written prayer, between the lines of your joys and concerns for the day, repeat this refrain: "God is with me!"

Experiencing Psalm 23

A walk "through the valley of the shadow of death" has poetic beauty
that does not resonate with my soul
and I resent being here.
I resist the chasm that is this heartache,
this devastation,
this loss.
I can only assume that the Shepherd's staff supports me
because I haven't fallen face-first
into any pools of still water.
If there are glorious green pastures in the valley
I cannot see them. Death has blinded me.
"Stay with me here, sit with me"
is the only prayer I can muster.
Let the house of the LORD be here
as long as the darkest valley
is my dwelling.
May a stream of oil make a path to find me
until I am healed and renewed
for the journey again.

God walks with you through dark valleys
and green pastures alike.

READ Psalm 23.

Surely the psalmist experienced some dark valleys and days of despair—and felt God's comforting presence through those difficult times—to be able to affirm his faith with such lyrical confidence! Yet we cannot always see God's goodness through the shadows. In your written prayer, do not be afraid to be fully honest with God about a source of pain or despair.

24   Uncertain

Dear Jesus, I hold out my hands, unclenched to show you the questions for which I have no answers: pain that is slow in healing, money woes without solution, the body deteriorating with age, intentional injury that defies logic or love or decency. Is "Jesus" the simple answer? Looking back, I see that you offered more puzzles than answers; that still seems to be true. So I will sit here, with palms open and unresolved prayers, O complex Jesus, if you will sit with me. This I ask, for lack of answers. Amen.

God is big enough for your questions.

READ Mark 14:36.

Pour out your questions, big and small, in your prayer-writing today; do not be afraid if the questions feel impossible or seem to go unanswered. Consider scattering your prayer around the page using single words or short phrases; let the remaining white space reflect the unknowns and uncertainties.

25 Feeling a Prayer

I pray with all of my senses, O Living God:

> *I pray with my eyes smiling at the sight of a robin resting briefly*
> *on the branch outside my window.*

> *I pray with my fingers kneading the warm fibers of the knitted hat*
> *that I snuggle onto my daughter's head before sending her off to school.*

> *I pray with my nose breathing deeply to catch the smell of mud*
> *rising with the morning dew.*

> *I pray with my tongue savoring the heavy spices of morning tea,*
> *a taste both comforting and awakening.*

> *I pray with my ears tuned to the radio's news, catching words*
> *to lift up in prayer: "death" "unemployment" "protest" "refugee."*

I pray with all of my senses when I cannot sense you at all:

> *when life's affairs look bleak to my eyes;*

> *when compassionate touch is absent;*

> *when the putrid smell of war escapes the sterilized news;*

> *when the taste of the day is bitter;*

> *when my ears cannot catch even a whisper of your word.*

I pray with all of my senses, O Living God.

Taste God's goodness!

READ Psalm 34:8.

Surely our senses are to be used for finding and enjoying God! In your written prayer, challenge yourself to seek and celebrate God with each of your senses.

Simply

O God my God
Here I am
It is only me
But it is all me
May it be enough
That is, enough of you
Because it is just me
But all you.

God will direct you.

READ 1 Samuel 3:1–10.

We are not alone when we struggle to hear and understand God's voice, or when we wonder what God wants us to do in our lives. Yet, quite possibly, God's answer to us is simpler than we expect. Let your written prayer seek God's direction to you for this day.

Focusing on Rocks

Thank you, God, for the vast beauty of nature—yes, thank you and amen—but today I want to give praise and say thanks for one specific piece within the splendor of your creation: rocks.

Thank you for rocks.

For pointed rocks that I dug up from the cornfields as a child, in search of arrowheads.

For climbable boulders on the islands of Maine where lupines bloom in abundance.

For rainbow layers of geological history exposed to travelers where hills have been cut open for roads to pass.

For smooth rocks, perfect for skipping across the river, scaring the geese that idle in the water.

For rocks (and seashells) worn down by centuries of waves to become grains of sand that invite wiggling toes.

For the Steadfast and Holy Rock that I claim beneath my feet, which is more beautiful than all other rocks.

Thank you for rocks.

The natural beauty of God is all around you.

READ Psalm 18:1–2.

Choose an aspect of nature that you particularly love: the wind moving through the tree branches, the sound of a waterfall, the birds gathered at the birdbath in your backyard. . . . Write a prayer of praise to God for this natural gift.

28 Unrequited

Still the end of the day comes, still the darkness falls and Orion rises, and a glass of wine does not draw me any closer to communion with You. I am torn between guilt-induced prayer to bridge this silent chasm . . . and mindless silence to turn prayerfully, painfully, away from what I cannot hear anyway. You are—*where?*—tonight, and I am here alone, here at a loss. Be in the darkness, I pray. Return me safely to sunlight.

God will listen to your fears.

READ Job 9:1–12.

Job dares to express his anger and pain when he feels that God is absent from the troubles of his life. In your written prayer, be honest about your fears or lost faith in God. You might begin with an echo of Job's words in verse 11, "Do not overlook me. . . ."

29 For a Moment, and a Lifetime

To you, O Christ, I bring thanksgiving
for warmth und humor and gentleness,
for your faithfulness to generations
and steadfast love rising with each dawn.
I lift up the delights of my life
knowing that grass fades and withers
yet longing for permanence in these moments.
To you I sing praise, to you I whisper fears;
I breathe in Julian of Norwich's prayer that all will be well
and all manner of things will be well.
So to you, O Christ, I pray with my ancestors
for daily bread and daily love
and that, in the end, all will be well.

Christ is the Bread of Life.

READ Matthew 6:9–13.

What is the "daily bread" that you need to live today fully, joyfully, with love and compassion? Pray for daily bread and blessing today.

Seeking Signs

Gideon felt dew on the fleece of wool.
Noah saw the bow of color arched in the sky.
Thomas touched the scars from the nails in Jesus' side.

We pray for signs.

The psalmist observed the deer at the stream.
Peter dreamed of animals, reptiles, birds lowered in a sheet.
Deep in Egypt, the Hebrews marked their doors with blood.

We pray for signs.

For Hezekiah's reassurance and healing, the shadows retreated.
A young woman bore a son for the hope of the people.
Daniel interpreted the handwriting on the wall.

How great are God's signs, how mighty God's wonders.
The kingdom of the Most High God is an everlasting kingdom,
and God's sovereignty is from generation to generation.

We pray for signs to this generation, to this world,
for the sake of your holy reputation in these days.

(includes Daniel 4:3, adapted)

God is full of dreams, and will inspire your own!

READ Daniel 4:1–8.

Do you ever pray to God about your dreams—your daydreams of ambition or your hopeful dreams for your loved ones, your recurring nightmares or your deepest fears? In your written prayer, let God worry about your dreams, and bless you with vision and reassurance.

31 Traveling

In praise of the I AM who was and is and will be:

On the wings of the eagle I soar to the high reaches of the mountains, to the desolate snows of Mount Everest and the trembling sides of Redoubt Volcano— and your fierce love is there.

On the currents of the ocean I sink past the bright and busy coral reef to the deep canyon of unimaginable glowing sea creatures—and your startling beauty is there.

On the rising steam of hot *ugali* and stewed goat meat I laugh with the crowd of bodies dancing and children weaving throughout—and your brilliant music is there.

On the pulsing beam of a lighthouse over Cape May Point I marvel at the seasons changing across land, bay, ocean, land, bay, ocean, land, bay, ocean—and your steadfast light is there.

God's Spirit will travel with you.

READ Psalm 36:5–9.

God's love and God's light extend to the horizons . . . and beyond! Pray for the places you will go today, whether around the corner or around the world; pray for the vision to see God in every place.

On "Good Friday" Kind of Days

When the light of this day is done,
can I be with you in the darkness?
Will you hold my hand through that darkest valley?

When I sit and observe the long shadow of the cross,
can you keep me company?
Will you watch with me while I consider death?

When my breath at last expires
(and nothing can prepare me for it, I am sure),
Will you send your Spirit to give me a new kind of breath?

Jesus, you spoke boldly in the face of death;
can you forgive me if I am not brave in that moment?
Will you promise that I can be with you on the other side?

I don't need fancy words of salvation
or misplaced sentiments about God's will
I just need someone to be there
because I will be scared
scared of what's ahead
scared of what I'm leaving behind

When I tremble before death, today or tomorrow,
can you stay with me?
Will you promise not to leave me?

God will watch over you.

READ Genesis 32:6–12.

Where do you most need God with you, for comfort and courage? Let your written prayer lay your worries and fears bare before the God of Abraham, Isaac and Jacob, trusting in God's steadfast love.

From God

Stop!

Where are you going in such a rush, child of mine?

Today I am having lunch at your home.

Today I am spending the day with you.

Today I've planned to sit with you and listen to your thoughts.

Today it's just you and me, reflecting together on life as good friends do.

Stop!

What are your thoughts? Where is your heart today, child after my own heart?

God will meet you in the stillness.

READ Luke 19:1–6.

The forty days are almost finished; are you still enjoying this time of seeking Jesus, or are you struggling to make time for prayer? Sit quietly in God's presence before picking up your pen. Use your written prayer to ask God to surround your day with holy stillness and peace.

Spring Rain

Rain down on me, blessed Creator,
rain down with mercy and grace
for the living of these days.

Rain down on me, blessed Savior,
rain down with love and strength
for the walking of this journey.

Rain down on me, blessed Breath,
rain down with holy fire and faith
for the empowering of your disciple.

God's blessings will rain down on you.

READ Genesis 2:4–14.

God has blessed the earth and blessed our lives with the gifts that we need for each day: dirt and rain, fruitful trees, breath for life. Praise God in your written prayer for God's abundance.

Praying with My Hands

I pray with these hands:
for the humility to remain open, unclenched;
for the gentleness to touch and care.
I pray with these hands cupped,
longing for a blessing.
I pray with my hands clasped,
fingers overlapping:
may they have something to hold onto.
I pray with my hands dirty from the day,
gratified but tired from the work,
asking for renewal.
I pray because my hands are at a loss,
fingers wide in uncertainty.
I fold my hands and pray
for the Word Made Flesh
to be holy in this flesh,
in these hands.

The Spirit is at work through our hands.

READ Matthew 8:1–3, 14–15.

It's amazing how much care can be communicated through a simple touch. Pray for the work of your hands today, that you will convey care and compassion along the way. Pray for the hands (and persons) working around the world to communicate God's strength and healing and protection.

Barren

O God, I come to you with my barrenness,
asking for new life beyond my imagining.
I wanted to create and dream, but I cannot.
I wanted to be filled with purpose, but I am not.
I wanted to begin a new journey, but my body is exhausted.
See, I am here in your temple
to make sure that you hear me.
I will not relent until you respond,
until you reveal another direction for my life.
I will come to you day after day
until you open a new door.
O God my God,
what options do I have?
Is my usefulness suddenly gone?
See how others are making a way for themselves,
but I have no way.
Look around and see
how those who sow and plant and harvest
are valued for their gifts to the community,
but my fields lie fallow and dry.
I have no place to call my own
just this square of floor in the temple
to lay out my pleas.
God of my mother and my mother's mother,
bless me with unexpected life and
surprising creativity, I pray.
To your glory.

God will answer your prayer.

READ 1 Samuel 1:9–18.

God is known for making a way out of no way . . . yet that doesn't always mean that we get what we want. Let your written prayer pour out a longing or deep sadness before the God of peace.

*O God, grant me clarity of thought
to make purposeful decisions,*

*deep joy in breathing
to pause and reflect,*

*generosity of heart
to love beyond my boundaries,*

*bravery in truth
to grow willingly,*

*strength for perseverance in faith
to experience grace amidst hardship,*

*and an endless spirit of prayer
to sustain me daily.*

God is the wellspring that nurtures your roots and strengthens your faith.

READ Ephesians 3:14–21.

Let your written prayer invite God's guidance and presence to keep you "rooted and grounded in love" (3:17, NRSV), both today and as you continually grow as a disciple of Christ.

Four Corners

Call to the east, to the west, to the north and the south!
Call to the ends of the earth for God's name to be lifted up:

> *God above all the gods*
> *Foundation for all lovingkindness*
> *Center of the orbits of galaxies*

Proclaim to the east, to the west, to the north and the south!
Proclaim to the ends of the earth that God has done it:

> *Rainmaker in seasons of drought*
> *Laughter in every friendship*
> *Nursing Breast to the hungry and the orphan*

Call to the east, to the west, to the north and the south!
Call to the ends of the earth for God's kingdom to take on flesh:

> *Mountain Guide to those lost and foraging*
> *Healing Touch to those on battlefields*
> *Sunlight to the plants' yearning branches*

Be gratified by our lives given over to your praise,
O God of our salvation!

God will continue to be revealed to you
in new images!

READ Revelation 21:22–23.

What are your favorite images of God? Jot them down around the page; then spend time with each image, adding words to describe how it makes you feel or writing a brief prayer for someone who comes to mind. (For example, I might start with REFRESHING SPIRIT and then add the words CALM, DEEP BREATH, AUTUMN BREEZE, and the prayer SWIRL AROUND LINDA WHO NEEDS A FRESH PERSPECTIVE.)

Confessional

With a deep breath and humility,
i bring my confessions to you, most gracious God:

How often i sit pretty on the promise of God's blessings
and disregard the unequivocal reprimand of Jesus' woes!

Woe to me when i petition God for luxuries
beyond daily bread.

Woe to me when i sacrifice care
for comfort.

Woe to me when i do not use my voice
for justice among neighbors and peace between enemies.

Woe to me when i provoke another's anger
and neglect to ask forgiveness from my brother.

Woe to me for my resentment
of life's strains and stresses.

Woe to me when i value order
over grace.

Woe to me for setting prestige and rapport
on pedestals toward which i strive.

Woe to me for believing that it is about me at all;
woe to me and glory to God, the source of all blessings.

Jesus will encourage you as you learn and change.

READ Luke 6:20–26.

Jesus often upsets our understandings of how the world works. Let your written prayer struggle with those things that don't make sense to you or that challenge your everyday routines and assumptions. You might begin with: "Teaching Jesus, there is so much that I don't understand. . . ."

Praise in Haiku

I trust in the dawn
to say "God lets you restart."
Praise the Morning Star!

Create in me a clean heart, O God.

I trust the fresh air
to feel the Spirit within.
Praise the Holy Wind!

Put a new and steadfast spirit within me.

I trust the spring buds
to stir my sense of oneness.
Praise the Mystery!

Restore to me the joy of your salvation.

I trust the mountain
to turn my heart to silence.
Praise the Restful Word!

Sustain in me a generous spirit.

(includes Psalm 51:10–12, adapted)

God will be compassionate.

READ Psalm 51.

We are not always comfortable making our prayers of confession to God, yet true confession trusts that God is good and loving and cares for us even at our worst. Let your written prayer trust God enough to confess a frustrating challenge or burden of guilt, and receive God's compassion and restoration.

PRAYERS AND PROMPTS
FOR HOLY WEEK

Palms and Passion

Rescue me, mighty Deliverer,
from my callousness to the world around me,
from my blind eye turned away from your world,
your people,
your pain.

Save me from dispassionate ears listening (without hearing) to news
of violence and hunger and despair, not recognizing
your call to engage my gifts in service
to participate in healing,
to partner with love.

Deliver me now from singing easy Hosannas with the crowd
but overlooking the dramatic passions of Holy Week:
money over faith, power over compassion,
and the ultimate struggles
of life and death.

Jesus will engage your mind, body,
and spirit this week.

READ Mark 11.

Holy Week is charged with passions and difficult lessons; it can be tempting to tune out the familiar drama without wrestling for deeper faith. Let your written prayer begin, "Saving God, give me courage to be wholly attentive. . . ."

Monday In Praise of Green

Praise God, on this spring morning, for the spectrum of greens!

Praise for the emerald of ivy climbing the dark tree bark!

Praise for the gray-green, almost blue, of onion grass sprouting tall!

Praise for the sunlit lime of new leaves budding on tall oaks!

Praise for the chartreuse of a tall iris just before the flower buds!

Praise for the lush olive grass underfoot in the early morning, soaked with dew!

Praise for the warm jade of an aloe vera sunning on my windowsill!

Praise God for the glorious array of vibrant greens!

All of creation praises its Creator!

READ Psalm 148.

The beauty of the earth often inspires our hearts to draw close to God. Can you take your writing outdoors today? Take a deep breath of the air, take in the beauty of the natural world (regardless of your location, rural or urban, lowlands or mountains). Use your written prayer to celebrate one of the stunning details of creation.

Enlightening

Be creativity when I am stagnant,
O God of the red-breasted robin and bright daffodil.

Be insight and direction when I spin my wheels,
O Jesus in whose dusty way I strive to walk.

Be laughter when I take myself too seriously,
O Spirit splashing in the rain puddles.

God will provide joy, even in the wilderness.

READ Jeremiah 31:2–13.

Imagine the words of your prayer dancing! Imagine a deep and joyful faith that makes your feet tap and skip! Even amidst the somber overtones of Holy Week, let your written prayer ring with joy!

John 11:35

What a life you have given us, God,

and who in the world can be expected to navigate it all?!

How many times can I cry as I absorb

the daily news of misunderstanding and distrust?

the reality of violence among family, of disparagement

among those who are supposed to love?

the pressure of success placed on the youngest among us?

the strain on us to be self-sufficient,

to not need and not ask?

Tell me, God, should I weep in despair

or laugh at the overwhelming absurdity of it all?

Jesus cried, at least once.

I think that I would cry more often than Jesus

but laughter is a cheerier mechanism to cope

with what I see

what I hear

what I feel

what I fear.

I don't know what you think of all the ceremony

we've given to this week called "Holy,"

but at the very least it gives us an outlet

for processing

suspense

doubt

death

fear

anger

complexity

and, hopefully, agreeing with you at the end of it all

that life is the most important thing,

Jesus understands your sadness, your hope, your humor, your fear!

worth laughing at and worth crying over.
Worth fighting for.
There's no navigating life without being scarred,
but there's grace for living with the scars.
There's grace.
There's grace.
My God, thank you for grace.

READ John 11:1–44.
Notice the range of emotions displayed in this text. Write a prayer of gratitude that God has given us emotion to experience humanity, and that God is God-enough to know our laughter and our tears alike.

Miserere

In the chilly early morning,
Have mercy on me, Son of the Living God.

In the waning evening light,
Have mercy on me, Son of the Living God.

In the nakedness of solitude,
Have mercy on me, Son of the Living God.

In the squall of daily decisions,
Have mercy on me, Son of the Living God.

In my regrets, in my triumphs,
Have mercy on me, Son of the Living God.

Sitting at your feast table amidst friends,
Have mercy on me, Son of the Living God.

Watching, waiting, at the foot of your cross,
Have mercy on me, Son of the Living God.

God is gracious.

READ Psalm 56.

Let your written prayer begin in imitation of the psalm, "Be gracious to me, O God . . ." (NRSV).

Darkness over the Land

Jesus. Jesus!
JESUS!
How could you let this happen?
Being with you was the most invigorating experience in the world
but now, now . . .
Now I would rather curl up into a cocoon
than face this death, face your blood.
Jesus. Jesus!
The bluebells ring silently in mourning.
They are stunned too.
Don't you see:
in the breath of a moment since the sun went out
the wars have escalated
the poor have abandoned hope
the woman has lost courage to knock on the judge's door
and the heartbroken cannot be comforted
because no one knows how.
JESUS!
We rejected and ridiculed you,
but why did you let this happen?
How could you leave us?

God remembers you—your name is inscribed
on God's hand.

READ Mark 15:33–34.

On this Good Friday, we do well to remember that Jesus is not the only one who feels forgotten: many feel the pangs of death, rejection, and loneliness on a daily basis. Reach out with compassion to others through your written prayer today. Consider sending copies of your prayer to certain friends who are experiencing Good Friday in a very personal way—with grief or desperation or hopelessness.

Between Hopelessness and Hope

Today I wait, at a loss,
Because everything I thought I knew
Everything I hoped for
Has died.

Today I have no prayers
Because what if it is God who took it all away?
I could not bear it,
So I do not ask.

Today there is nothing to do
But sit in silence. And breathe. And stare
At the rock face of the tomb
And wonder about endings.

God will come when you wait patiently.

READ 1 Kings 19:11–13.

How often do we meet God in the place, at the time, that we least expect?! Watch for God with Elijah today, beginning your written prayer with the words of today's prayer, "Today I wait. . . ."

Amen

And so Lent comes to its end,
Easter marks the completion,
and I pray, O most holy God,
for what is, in fact, a beginning:
life new and renewing;
the impossible to be believed;
joy that cannot be quenched;
and always,
everywhere I look
every place I turn,
your endless love and grace.
Amen and amen!

Jesus is Life!

READ 2 Corinthians 1:19–20.

Easter is God's dramatic "Yes!" to life. Let your written prayer celebrate God's gift of life, affirming God's "Yes!" with your own "Amen!"

Acknowledgments

I greatly appreciate the team at Paraclete Press who received this book with enthusiasm and a ready understanding of embodied prayer, and Jon Sweeney for his editing eye and creative vision.

I offer endless thanks to my family for their love, support and encouragement. Noah and Faith, thank you for being proud of your mom and her book—I am tremendously proud of you both! I am indebted to my sister, Naomi Hackenberg, who shared her time and professional expertise with me at each step of this book's process.

I'm grateful to the community of Grace United Church of Christ in Lancaster, Pennsylvania for being a sacred space where each person—including the pastor—is empowered to share her/his spiritual gifts and talents, and to the members of the "Praying Through My Pen" small group at Grace who have written with me weekly for the past two years!

Index of Scriptural Praying Prompts

About Paraclete Press

Who We Are

Paraclete Press is a publisher of books, recordings, and DVDs on Christian spirituality. Our publishing represents a full expression of Christian belief and practice—from Catholic to Evangelical, from Protestant to Orthodox.

We are the publishing arm of the Community of Jesus, an ecumenical monastic community in the Benedictine tradition. As such, we are uniquely positioned in the marketplace without connection to a large corporation and with informal relationships to many branches and denominations of faith.

What We Are Doing

Books

Paraclete publishes books that show the richness and depth of what it means to be Christian. Although Benedictine spirituality is at the heart of all that we do, we publish books that reflect the Christian experience across many cultures, time periods, and houses of worship. We publish books that nourish the vibrant life of the church and its people—books about spiritual practice, formation, history, ideas, and customs.

We have several different series, including the best-selling Paraclete Essentials, and Paraclete Giants series of classic texts in contemporary English; A Voice from the Monastery—men and women monastics writing about living a spiritual life today; award-winning literary faith fiction and poetry; and the Active Prayer Series that brings creativity and liveliness to any life of prayer.

Recordings

From Gregorian chant to contemporary American choral works, our music recordings celebrate sacred choral music through the centuries. Paraclete distributes the recordings of the internationally acclaimed choir Gloriæ Dei Cantores, praised for their "rapt and fathomless spiritual intensity" by *American Record Guide*, and the Gloriæ Dei Cantores Schola, which specializes in the study and performance of Gregorian chant. Paraclete is also the exclusive North American distributor of the recordings of the Monastic Choir of St. Peter's Abbey in Solesmes, France, long considered to be a leading authority on Gregorian chant.

DVDs

Our DVDs offer spiritual help, healing, and biblical guidance for life issues: grief and loss, marriage, forgiveness, anger management, facing death, and spiritual formation.

Learn more about us at our website:
www.paracletepress.com, or call us toll-free at 1-800-451-5006.

Also in the "Active Prayer Series"

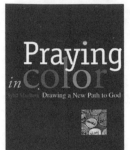

Praying in Color: *Drawing a New Path to God*
Sybil MacBeth

ISBN: 9781557255129
$16.95, Paperback

If you are word-weary, stillness-challenged, easily distracted, or just in need of a new way to pray, give this book a try.

Praying with the Body: *Bringing the Psalms to Life*
Roy De Leon

ISBN: 9781557255891
$16.99, Paperback

This book is an invitation to move in prayer by expressing the psalms with motion.

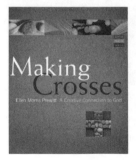

Making Crosses: *A Creative Connection to God*
Ellen Morris Prewitt

ISBN: 9781557256287
$16.99, Paperback

The practice of making a cross takes you beyond analytic thinking and offers a way of prayer where understanding comes from doing.

Available from most booksellers or through Paraclete Press
www.paracletepress.com
1-800-451-5006
Try your local bookstore first.